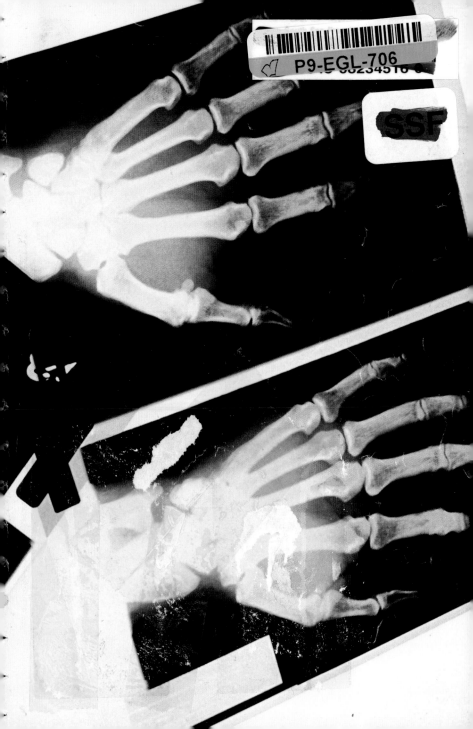

Your 206 Bones, 32 Teeth, and Other Body Math

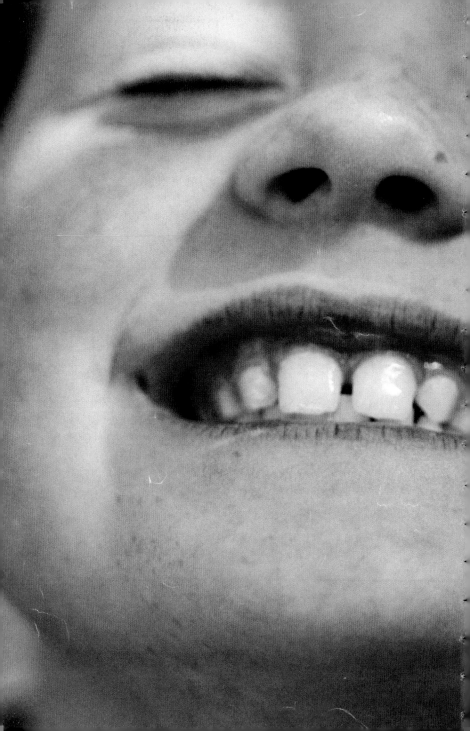

Your 206 Bones, 32 Teeth, *and* Other Body Math

By Robyn O'Sullivan

NATIONAL GEOGRAPHIC

WASHINGTON D.C.

One of the world's largest nonprofit scientific and educational organizations, the National Geographic Society was founded in 1888 "for the increase and diffusion of geographic knowledge." Fulfilling this mission, the Society educates and inspires millions every day through its magazines, books, television programs, videos, maps and atlases, research grants, the National Geographic Bee, teacher workshops, and innovative classroom materials. The Society is supported through membership dues, charitable gifts, and income from the sale of its educational products. This support is vital to National Geographic's mission to increase global understanding and promote conservation of our planet through exploration, research, and education.

For more information, please call
1-800-NGS-LINE (647-5463) or write to the following address:
National Geographic Society
1145 17th Street N.W.
Washington, D.C. 20036-4688
U.S.A.

For information about special discounts for bulk purchases, please contact
National Geographic Books Special Sales at ngspecsales@ngs.org

Visit the Society's Web site: www.nationalgeographic.com

Library of Congress Cataloging-in-Publication Data

O'Sullivan, Robyn.
  Your 206 bones, 32 teeth, and other body math / by Robyn O'Sullivan.
    p. cm. -- (National Geographic science chapters)
  Includes bibliographical references and index.
  ISBN-13: 978-0-7922-5955-8 (library binding)
  ISBN-10: 0-7922-5955-6 (library binding)
  1. Body, Human. 2. Mathematics. I. Title. II. Title: Your two hundred six bones, thirty-two teeth, and other body math. III. Series.
  QP38.O884 2006
  612--dc22

2006016317

Photo Credits
Front Cover: © Firefly Productions/Corbis; Spine: © Corbis; Endpaper: © Corbis; 2-3: © Joel Sartore/ National Geographic Image Collection; 6: © PhotoDisc/ Getty Images; 7: © Jose Azel/ Aurora/ Getty Images; 8: © John Kelly/ The Image Bank/ Getty Images; 10: 3D4Medical.com/ Getty Images; 11 (top): © Robert Warren/ Taxi/ Getty Images; 11 (bottom): © Digital Vision/ Getty Images; 13: © DK Images; 14: © Franco Vogt; 15: © Mediscan/ Visuals Unlimited; 16-17: © Frank Siteman/ Stone/ Getty IMages; 18 (right): © Yellow Dog Productions/ Taxi/ Getty Images; 19: © David Turnley/ Corbis; 20: © Pascal Rondeau/ Allsport Concepts/ Getty Images; 21: © 3D4Medical.com/ Getty Images; 22 (top): © Richard Price/ Getty Images; 22 (bottom): © PhotoDisc/ Getty Images; 23: © Lindsay Edwards Photography; 24: © Robert Cianflone/ Reportage/ Getty Images; 25: © Norbert Schoefer/ Corbis; 26: © Oxford Scientific Films; 27: © PhotoDisc/ Getty Images; 28: © Andy Caulfield/ Photographer's Choice/ Getty Images; 30: © Lisa Spindler Photography Inc/ Photonica/ Getty Images; 31: © Sean Justice/ Taxi/ Getty Images; 32: © Getty Images; 33: © Myrleen Ferguson Cate/ PhotoEdit; 34: © Ty Allison/ Getty Images; 35: © Stockdisc Classic/ Getty Images.

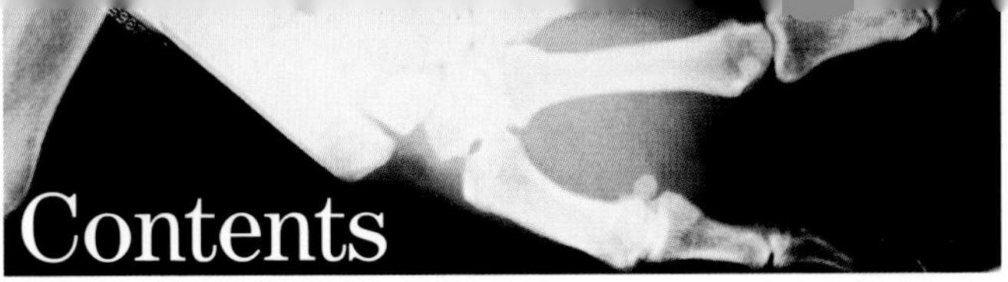

Contents

Introduction
Numbers and You   7

Chapter 1
An Amazing Machine   9

Chapter 2
On the Move   13

Chapter 3
Without a Thought   21

Chapter 4
Here's Looking at You   29

Chapter 5
Measuring the Things You Do   35

Report Guide   36

Glossary   38

Further Reading   39

Index   40

Measuring your height is just one way you can use numbers to describe your body.

Numbers and You

If you were asked to use numbers to tell about your body, what would you say? You might tell how much you weigh or how tall you are. Or you might say you have two eyes, one nose, ten fingers, and ten toes.

These are just a few of the ways you could use numbers to tell about your body. Let's find other numbers that can tell about you!

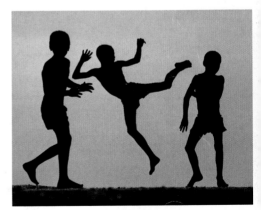

Our bodies are amazing
machines that enable us to
do all the things we do.

Chapter 1

An Amazing Machine

The human body is an amazing machine. It is made up of many parts that work together to keep you alive and active. We can use numbers to better understand how our bodies work.

75 Trillion (75,000,000,000,000) Cells

Like other living things, the human body is made up of cells—lots and lots of cells. These building blocks of life work together to create you and enable you to do all the things you do. Scientists estimate that an adult's body is made up of more than 75 trillion cells.

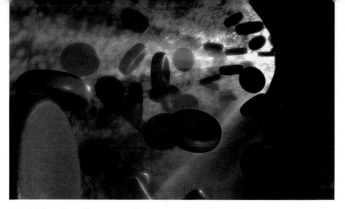

Red blood cells can only be seen with a mircroscope.

Not all of these cells are the same. The body is made up of blood cells, skin cells, nerve cells, and other types of cells. Each type of cell has a job to do.

10 Systems

Cells that work together to do a specific job are called organs. Your heart is an organ. So are your lungs. Organs that work together form systems that perform major tasks for your body. For example, your brain and your nerves work together to tell your body what to do. They make up your nervous system. Your nervous system is one of ten systems in your body.

Ten Systems in the Body

1. The nervous system controls the body.

2. The muscular system makes movement possible.

3. The skeletal system supports the body.

4. The circulatory system moves blood throughout the body.

5. The respiratory system provides the body with oxygen.

6. The digestive system breaks down food into nutrients.

7. The excretory system gets rid of waste.

8. The immune system protects the body against disease and infection.

9. The endocrine system regulates the body's functions.

10. The reproductive system enables people to produce offspring.

If it weren't for her bones and muscles, this girl couldn't do karate or any other sport.

Chapter 2

On the Move

If it weren't for your bones and muscles, you wouldn't be able to stand up, let alone move. But these body parts make action possible. They enable you to get up and go.

206 Bones

Imagine your body without bones. You wouldn't be able to stand up! That's because your bones form a frame called a skeleton. Your skeleton gives your body shape.

▶ The bones in your body fit together to form a skeleton.

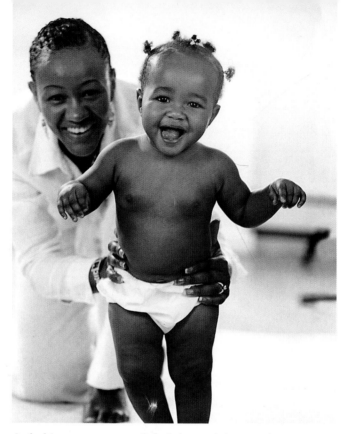

As babies grow, some of their bones join together.

Did you know that babies have more bones in their bodies than adults? Newborn babies have 300 bones in their bodies, but adults only have 206. How can that be? As babies grow, some of their bones join together. That's why adults have fewer bones than babies.

Some bones protect parts of your body.
Run your fingers along the sides of your
belly. Can you feel your ribs? Your ribs are
like a cage of bones in your chest. They
protect your heart and lungs.

Other bones work with muscles so you
can move. The bones in your feet and legs
help you to stand up and walk. The bones in
your hands and fingers help you to pick
things up.
Your thigh
bone, or
femur, is the
longest bone
in your body.
The smallest
bone in your
body is in
your ear.

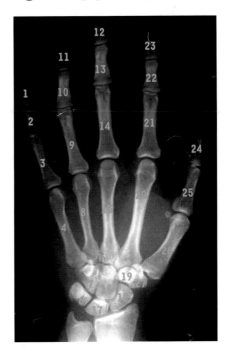

An x-ray shows
the 27 bones in
your hand.

Over 230 Joints

Our bones support our bodies, but we couldn't bend if it weren't for joints. The places where two or more bones meet are called joints. Your body has more than 230 joints that allow your body to move in different ways.

The joint at your elbow is a hinge joint. This type of joint enables you to bend your arm back and forth in one direction. If it weren't for this type of joint, you couldn't lift things.

The joints in your neck are pivot joints. They allow you to turn your head from side to side without turning your entire body.

Your shoulders and hips are both ball-and-socket joints. In these types of joints, a ball

Joints enable us to move in different ways.

at the end of one bone fits into a rounded
area at the end of another bone. Ball-and-
socket joints allow you to move your arms
and legs in an almost limitless number
of directions.

660 Muscles

Bones and joints provide you with support and flexibility, but it's the muscles attached to your bones that make movement possible. There are about 660 muscles in the human body. Most of them work in pairs. Different kinds of muscles do different things.

People use 43 muscles when they frown, but it only takes 17 muscles to smile.

A boy uses a lot of different muscles in gym class.

The muscles in your legs help you walk. Your arm muscles help you throw a ball or pick something up. But muscles aren't all about lifting things or even walking. You use your muscles every time you speak and even when you smile. You control the muscles you use to walk and talk. Your brain tells these muscles what to do.

Playing sports causes your
heart to beat faster.

Without a Thought

You've just read about muscles that you control. Your body also has muscles that work by themselves. These muscles do vital jobs without you having to give it a thought.

100,800 Heartbeats

Your heart is a muscle. It pumps blood throughout your body. Your heart beats about 70 times a minute. That's 4,200 times an hour, and 100,800 times a day! Your heart works this hard without ever stopping to rest.

▶ Your heart is about the size of your fist.

A doctor uses a stethoscope to hear your heart beat.

Your pumping heart circulates your blood throughout your body about three times every minute. The blood travels in tubes called blood vessels.

▶ Arteries and veins carry blood throughout your body.

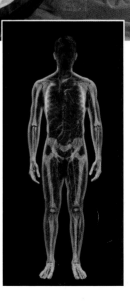

Blood vessels called arteries carry oxygen-rich blood away from your heart. Veins carry the blood back to your heart. All together, there are more than 60,000 miles (96,558 km) of blood vessels in your body.

You can't see the blood in your body. But you can feel your heart beating in your chest. You can also feel blood pumping through some of your blood vessels. This is called your pulse. The easiest places to feel your pulse are on your neck and your wrist. Place two fingers on the back of your wrist and count how many times you feel a beat in a minute.

You can use two fingers to measure your pulse. How many times does your heart beat in a minute?

23

You breathe in air through your mouth and nose.

1,800 Breaths

When you breathe, your two lungs take in oxygen from the air. People need oxygen to make their bodies work. Children breathe about 30 times a minute when resting, or sitting still. That means they take about 1,800 breaths in an hour.

Your lungs work like sponges. Except instead of soaking up water, they soak up the oxygen that's in the air you breathe. The oxygen is then passed to the blood that circulates through your body. The blood takes the oxygen to all the cells in your body.

When you exercise, you breathe faster. When you run or swim, you might breathe 60 times in a minute. You breathe faster because your body needs more oxygen.

We breathe faster when we are active.

1,500 Blinks

Most people blink about 25 times every minute. That's about 1,500 times every hour. Every time you blink, tears come out of your upper eyelids. The eyelids spread the tears across your eyes as you blink. The tears wash away germs and dirt in your eyes. The tears also keep your eyes from drying out.

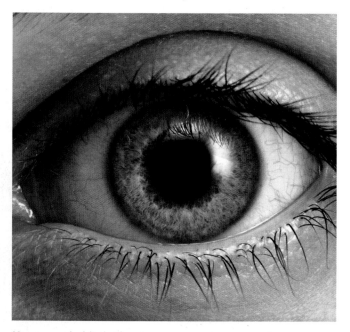

Most people blink about once every two seconds.

Your eyes would dry out if they stayed open all the time.

Here's Looking at You

You've seen how numbers can be used to describe how your body works. Numbers can also be used to talk about how your body looks.

Nine Pounds of Skin

If you rub your hands on your cheeks, what do you feel? Skin. Skin covers your cheeks and the rest of your body, too. In fact, your skin is your largest and heaviest organ. The average adult's skin weighs nine pounds (4 kg).

When a baby tooth falls out, it makes room for an adult tooth.

Your skin has many important jobs to do. Your skin protects your organs, bones, and muscles, and it keeps germs out of your body. Your skin also helps control your body temperature.

Skin can be many different colors.

Your skin is packed full of nerve endings. They allow you to feel the things you touch. Thanks to the nerves in your skin, you can feel textures, heat, and pain.

The color of your skin is determined by the amount of melanin in your skin. Melanin is a pigment, or color. Dark-skinned people have more melanin in their skin than people with light skin.

100,000 Hairs

How many hairs do you have on your head? Most people have about 100,000 hairs on their head. Hair keeps your head warm. It also helps to protect the skin on your head from the sun's dangerous rays.

Hair grows about half an inch every month. Hair grows out of follicles. These are small tubes in the skin. When a hair finishes growing, it falls out. Then a new hair grows from the follicle.

Each hair grows out of a hair follicle beneath the skin.

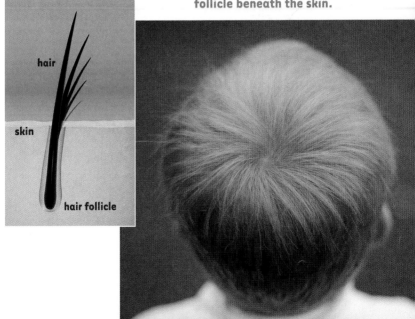

hair

skin

hair follicle

32 Teeth

What would you do without teeth? You use your teeth to bite and chew food. Teeth also help you to talk clearly. They help shape many of the sounds in your mouth when you talk.

Most children lose their front teeth when they are six or seven years old.

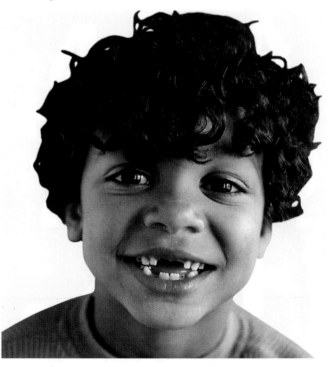

We use our teeth to break food into bite-sized pieces.

Most adults have 32 teeth. However, they don't have 32 teeth their entire lives. Babies are born with 20 teeth inside their gums. The teeth start to push through the gums when a baby is about six months old. When a child is about six years old, these baby teeth start to fall out. They are replaced by the adult teeth that grow in behind them.

Chapter 7

Measuring the Things You Do

Besides measuring your body and its various parts, you can also measure many things your body can do. For example, how fast can you run? How high can you jump? How long can you hold your breath? Get a stopwatch and a measuring tape and find out. What else can you count or measure about the human body?

◀ Can you jump high enough to block a shot?

How to Write an A+ Report

1. Choose a topic.
- Find something that interests you.
- Make sure it is not too big or too small.

2. Find sources.
- Ask your librarian for help.
- Use many different sources: books, magazine articles, and websites.

3. Gather information.
- Take notes. Write down the big ideas and interesting details.
- Use your own words.

4. Organize information.
- Sort your notes into groups that make sense.

- Make an outline. Put your groups of notes in the order you want to write your report.

5. Write your report.

- Write an introduction that tells what the report is about.

- Use your outline and notes as you write to make sure you say everything you want to say in the order you want to say it.

- Write an ending that tells about your report.

- Write a title.

6. Revise and edit your report.

- Read your report to make sure it makes sense.

- Read it again to check spelling, punctuation, and grammar.

7. Hand in your report!

Glossary

blood vessel   a tube that carries blood inside your body

cell   the smallest unit of life

follicle   a small tube under the skin out of which a hair can grow

germ   a tiny living thing that can cause disease

heart   the organ in the human body that pumps blood

joint   the place where two bones meet

lung   one of two organs that make breathing possible

melanin   the pigment or color in our skin that determines our skin color

organ   a body part that performs a specific function for the body

oxygen   a gas that is part of the air we breathe

pulse   the pumping of blood through our blood vessels

skeleton   all the bones of a body connected together

system   organs that work together to perform a major task for the human body

Further Reading

• Books •

Beres, Samantha. *101 Things Every Kid Should Know About the Human Body*. Los Angeles, CA: Lowell House Juvenile, 2000. Ages 9-12, 28 pages.

Davidson, Dr. Sue and Ben Morgan. *Human Body Revealed*. New York, NY: DK Publishing, 2002. Ages 9-12, 38 pages.

Incredible Voyage: Exploring the Human Body. Washington, DC: National Geographic Society, 2003. Ages 13-adult, 352 pages.

Parker, Steve. *How the Body Works*. Chappaqua, NY: Reader's Digest, 1999. Ages 9-12, 192 pages.

Rowan, Dr. Pete. *Some Body*. New York, NY: Alfred A. Knopf, 1995. Ages 9-12, 44 pages.

Weiner, Esther. *The Incredible Human Body*. New York, NY: Scholastic, 2000. Ages 9-12, 96 pages.

• Websites •

British Broadcasting Company (BBC)
http://www.bbc.co.uk/science/humanbody/

Discovery
http://yucky.kids.discovery.com/body/

Discovery Kids
http://www.discoverykids.ca/gross/systems/systems.asp

Enchanted Learning
http://www.enchantedlearning.com/subjects/anatomy/titlepage.shtml

Human Anatomy Online
http://www.innerbody.com/index.html

Kids Health
http://www.kidshealth.org/kid/body/mybody.html

ThinkQuest
http://library.thinkquest.org/J0111100/

Wikipedia Encyclopedia
http://en.wikipedia.org/wiki/Human_body

Index

blood vessel 22, 23, 38

bone 12–18, 30

breath 24, 25

cell 9, 10, 25, 38

eye 26, 27

eyelid 26

follicle 31, 38

germ 26, 30, 38

hair 31

heart 10, 15, 20–23, 38

heartbeat 21, 23

joint 16–18, 38

lung 10, 15, 24, 38

melanin 30, 38

muscle 12, 13, 15, 18, 19,
                                            21, 30

organ 10, 29, 30, 38

oxygen 11, 24, 25, 38

pulse 23, 38

skeleton 11, 13, 38

skin 29, 30

system 10, 11, 38

teeth 29, 32, 33

x-ray 15

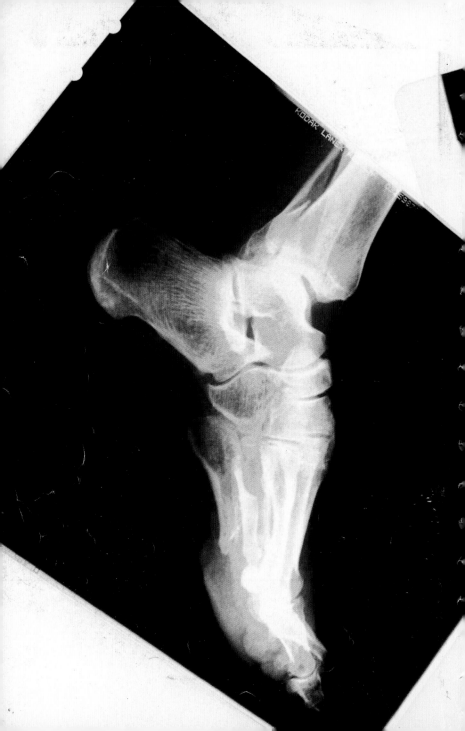